S0-ACU-667

Livonia Public Library
CARL SANDBURG BRANCH #21
30100 W. 7 Mile Road
Livonia, Mich. 48152
248-893-4010

JBIOG
ROBINSON
MAY 1 4 2013

WITHDRAWN

JACKIE
Robinson
AMERICAN HERO

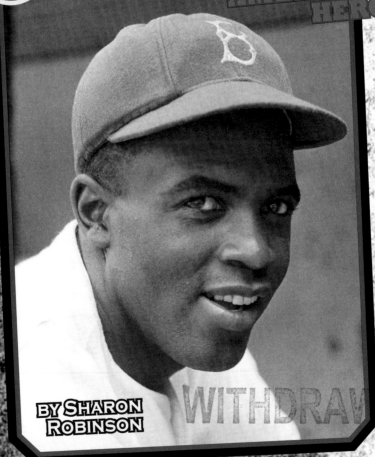

BY SHARON
ROBINSON

SCHOLASTIC INC.

Photo Credits: 3 top left (both): Photozek07/Dreamstime; 4–5 top: surawach5/Shutterstock; 4 bottom left and bottom right: Sports Illustrated/Getty Images; 5 bottom left: Sports Illustrated/Getty Images, bottom right: Time & Life Pictures/Getty Images; 17 bottom: Bettmann/Corbis; 22 bottom: Bettmann/Corbis; 27: Bettmann/Corbis; 30 bottom: Bettmann/Corbis; 33: Bettmann/Corbis; 35: Bettmann/Corbis; 41: Associated Press; 42: Associated Press; 45 top: Courtesy of Peter Simon; 46: Courtesy of Peter Simon.

All other photographs courtesy of the Jackie Robinson family.

No part of this publication may be reproduced, stored in a retrieval system, or transmitted in any form or by any means, electronic, mechanical, photocopying, recording, or otherwise, without written permission of the publisher. For information regarding permission, write to Scholastic Inc., Attention: Permissions Department, 557 Broadway, New York, NY 10012.

Copyright © 2013 by Sharon Robinson

All rights reserved. Published by Scholastic Inc. *Publishers since 1920.* SCHOLASTIC and associated logos are trademarks and/or registered trademarks of Scholastic Inc.

Library of Congress Cataloging-in-Publication Data

Robinson, Sharon, 1950–
Jackie Robinson : American hero / by Sharon Robinson. — Reinforced library binding.
pages cm
ISBN 978-0-545-56915-6
1. Robinson, Jackie, 1919–1972—Juvenile literature. 2. Baseball players—United States—Biography—Juvenile literature. 3. African American baseball players—Biography—Juvenile literature. I. Title.
GV865.R6R593 2013
796.357092—dc23
[B]
2012046058

10 9 8 7 6 5 4 3 2 1   13 14 15 16 17

Printed in the U.S.A.   141
First printing, March 2013

Designed by Liz Herzog

3 9082 12212 6439

CONTENTS

INTRODUCTION

The Brooklyn Dodgers faced the New York Yankees in the 1955 World Series. It was the top of the eighth inning in Game One and the Dodgers trailed the Yankees 4–6, with two outs. Jackie Robinson danced off third base. He was going to try to steal home.

Yankee pitcher Whitey Ford wound up. The second he looked away, Jackie tore down the third-base path. In

a dramatic finish, Jackie slid into home plate as Yankee catcher Yogi Berra dived to tag him out.

"Safe!" The umpire shouted.

"He's out!" Yogi screamed.

This memorable play is still hotly debated, but it illustrates Jackie's determination to win. The Dodgers lost that game, but won the series. They couldn't have done it without Jackie. On the field, he had the heart of a champion. Off the field, Jackie Robinson is an American hero.

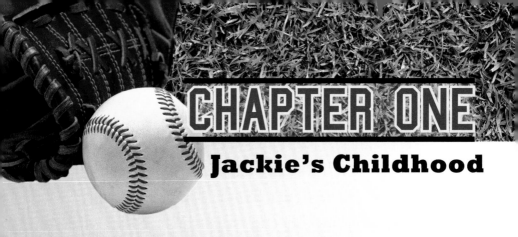

CHAPTER ONE

Jackie's Childhood

Jack Roosevelt Robinson was born on January 31, 1919, in a small cabin on the Sasser farm near Cairo, Georgia. He was the youngest of five: Edgar, Frank, Mack, and Willa Mae. His parents, Mallie and Jerry Robinson, were **sharecroppers**. His grandparents, Wash and Edna McGriff, were former slaves, but now owned their own farm.

Jackie grew up with **segregation** in America. Black and white people went to different schools, churches, and hospitals, and lived in separate neighborhoods. Black people drank from different water fountains, used separate bathrooms, and sat in different sections on buses, trains, and in movie theaters.

Jackie never knew his father. Jerry Robinson left the family when Jackie was only six months old. Unable to farm alone and care for her children, Mallie decided to follow her brother, Burton Thomas, to Pasadena, California.

Pasadena was beautiful. Mallie found work as a maid and a place to live with her brother. There were times when the family barely had enough money for food. The children ate food their mother brought home from work. Sometimes they ate only two meals a day. When there was no food in the house, the children soaked bread in sugar water.

Mallie found a second job to make more money. She saved enough to buy a house with her cousin Sam Wade. The house she wanted to buy was in an all-white neighborhood. Mallie knew the owner would not sell to a black family. So she sent a cousin, who looked white, to buy 121 Pepper Street. The neighbors were surprised when a black family moved into the house. Some of them tried to get the Robinsons to move out of the neighborhood by treating them badly. They burned a cross on the front lawn. They called the police regularly with complaints about the children. Once, Jackie's brother Edgar was arrested for roller-skating too fast!

At age eight, Jackie got into a screaming match with a white girl across the street. The girl's father threw stones at Jackie. But still Mallie refused to move.

In time, Mallie's kindness toward others won over most of her neighbors. The Robinsons called their big house "the castle." Jackie helped his mother plant a garden, feed the chickens, and water the fruit trees.

It was a rule that the older children took care of the younger ones. Jackie's sister, Willa Mae, took care of him. When she went to school, Jackie tagged along. Willa Mae would put Jackie in the sandbox outside her classroom. Jackie had to stay there until the kids came outside to play. They all wanted Jackie on their team because he was so good at every game. Some kids even gave him their lunch just so he'd play with them.

By the time Jackie was in third grade he was putting together sports teams. "We got a soccer team together," he once explained, "that was so good we challenged the sixth grade and beat them."

Mallie taught her children lessons from the Bible. One of her favorites was: "You must reap what you sow, so sow well!" Meaning, you'll be rewarded for working hard.

CHAPTER TWO

The Teen Years

Jackie loved his mother very much. He wanted to make her happy, but he sometimes got into trouble with his friends in the Pepper Street Gang. They were a bunch of black, Japanese, and Mexican boys who got into mischief. They'd throw dirt balls at passing cars, snatch balls from golf courses, and grab fruit from markets.

A young minister helped Jackie and his friends stay away from trouble. His name was Reverend Karl Downs. Reverend Downs met the boys on the basketball court. He invited the boys to his church, where they had sports and after-school programs for kids. Jackie and Reverend Downs stayed friends for life. In fact, Reverend Downs later married Jackie and his wife! But that's getting ahead of the story.

As teens, Jackie and his brothers Edgar and Mack were local star athletes. Edgar was a roller skater who was known to jump over the hoods of cars and race buses thirty miles from Pasadena to Santa Monica.

Mack was a sprinter and champion broad jumper. In the 1936 Olympics in Berlin, Germany, he ran the 200-meter dash in 21.1 seconds, finishing four tenths of a second behind the gold medalist, Jesse Owens.

In high school, Jackie was the quarterback for the Muir Terriers, the top shooter on the basketball team, a broad jumper, and a tennis champion.

At Pasadena Junior College (PJC), Jackie rushed for a 104-yard touchdown and was named Most Valuable Player. Another time, he set a record for competing in two different sports in two different cities on the same day. In the morning, Jackie was in Pomona, where he set a new broad-jump record of 25 feet 6½ inches. That afternoon, he played shortstop for PJC in Glendale and helped bring them a championship!

In February 1939, Jackie transferred to the

University of California at Los Angeles (UCLA) where he again **lettered** in four sports: football, basketball, baseball, and track.

Sportswriters called Robinson an unstoppable halfback; the best man on the basketball team; and a flawless shortstop. Jackie also set a record of 25 feet in the broad jump. And, he was the first UCLA student ever to letter in four sports in the same season!

Over the summer of 1940, Jackie's favorite brother, Frank, was killed in a motorcycle accident. After that tragedy, Mallie bought a smaller house and a sad Jackie returned to UCLA for his last year.

Jackie once said that he didn't think anything could come into his life that would be more important than sports. He felt that way until his friend Ray Bartlett introduced him to Rachel Isum. They met in the student lounge at UCLA. Rachel was a beautiful seventeen-year-old freshman in UCLA's nursing program.

Jackie was a senior and a star athlete. He admired Rachel's determination to graduate from college because not many black women went to college at that time. She liked that Jackie was down-to-earth.

Rachel lived at home in West Los Angeles with her parents, Zellee and Raymond Isum, and younger brother, Ray.

Rachel (middle) graduated from UC San Francisco.

Her older brother, Charles Williams, lived a few blocks away at their grandmother's house. Rachel's father was a disabled World War I veteran. Rachel was very close to him. Each summer, Raymond took the family camping at Lake Elsinore. It was during these trips that Rachel learned to love nature and water. Raymond died during Rachel's first year in college.

Zellee ran a catering business. She was the one who introduced nursing and music to Rachel. Zellee also taught her daughter the importance of hard work and setting goals. In fact, Rachel started working for her mother when she was ten.

When Rachel was a teenager, she began to help out at her grandparents' restaurant in Nogales, Arizona, a small town on the border with Mexico. One scary night, her grandmother, Annetta Jones, ran off a robber with her shotgun!

The spring after he met Rachel, Jackie told her that he was leaving UCLA before graduating.

Rachel with her younger brother, Ray.

Rachel's dad, with a friend, loving his new car.

They talked it over. Rachel accepted Jackie's decision. He signed on with a semiprofessional football team, the Honolulu Bears. He played one season and was in the middle of the Pacific Ocean aboard a ship bound for California when the Japanese bombed Pearl Harbor. This was the start of World War II for the United States.

CHAPTER THREE

A Black and White War

Like millions of American men, Jackie's fate was sealed. He arrived home to his **draft** letter and entered the army. Jackie completed basic training at Fort Riley, Kansas. He applied for Officer Candidate School (OCS) but was rejected. OCS did not accept black soldiers. Three months later, they changed their minds. Jackie and several other blacks were admitted into OCS training. Jackie graduated January 28, 1943, with the rank of second lieutenant.

After graduating from OCS, Jackie visited Rachel in San Francisco. She was completing the last two years of nursing training there, at the University of California. On this visit, Jackie and Rachel became engaged. They planned to marry after Rachel finished college and Jack was out of the service.

A happy man, Jackie headed back to Fort Riley, where he was named morale officer of his company. A year later, he was sent to the 761st Tank Battalion at Camp Hood, Texas. He was back in the South, where **Jim Crow laws** still kept blacks and whites separated. Even the army base was segregated. Black soldiers lived in a separate area. The Black officers even had a separate OCS and officers' club.

One day, Jackie was on a trip from the army base into town. He questioned the Jim Crow law that made blacks sit in the back of the bus. Jackie got on the bus and headed to the back of the bus when he spotted a friend, Virginia Jones. He sat down in the middle of the bus, next to Virginia. The driver ordered Jackie to move to the back of the bus. Jackie didn't move. Even though the army was segregated, he knew that the army had changed its policy and no longer allowed segregation on its military bases. Jackie also knew that boxing champions Joe Louis and Sugar Ray Robinson had recently refused to obey

Jim Crow laws at a bus station in Alabama. Jackie and the bus driver argued over his refusal to move. The driver stopped the bus near the military police station. He stormed off the bus and insisted that the military police arrest Jackie.

Jackie was taken to the guard house. Captain Gerald M. Bear, who was in charge of the military police, was called. Jackie and Captain Bear each claimed they had been disrespected. Captain Bear eventually brought a **court martial** against Jackie.

The case went before the military court. Jackie was accused of two counts of **insubordination** and disrespect toward Captain Bear, his superior officer. Jackie's lawyer brought in character witnesses who said that he was an excellent soldier and proved that many of the charges against his client were false. The court found Jackie not guilty. All charges against him were dismissed.

A few months later, Jackie put in a request to be placed on inactive duty. In October, he was honorably discharged from the army.

CHAPTER FOUR

Breaking the Color Barrier

The color barrier in Major League Baseball was not a written law, like the Jim Crow laws. But it still kept the races separated. If you were white, you played baseball on a team in Major League Baseball. If you had black or brown skin, you played baseball in the Negro Leagues.

After his army discharge, Jackie learned that one of the top Negro League teams, the Kansas City Monarchs, was looking for players. He wanted a chance to play ball professionally, so he tried out for the Monarchs. Jackie won a spot as shortstop on the team with stars such as Satchel Paige, Cool Papa Bell, and John "Buck" O'Neil.

Jackie proved to be a solid player. In his first season with the Monarchs, he was voted onto their all-star team. But Jackie didn't like the unfair color barrier. Buck O'Neil recalled one night when the Monarchs' bus pulled into a gas station; Jackie got off the bus to use the restroom. The station attendant told him to get back on the bus. Jackie hesitated, then told the attendant that if they couldn't use the bathroom, they'd get their gas somewhere else. When the station attendant thought about the money he'd lose, he backed down. He told the players to go ahead and be quick.

After the war, there was pressure on Major League Baseball to end segregation within the sport. It took one man from within baseball to take the first step. His name was Branch Rickey.

As president and general manager of the Brooklyn Dodgers, Mr. Rickey had made other bold moves in baseball. He'd founded the **farm team** system. Branch felt that segregation was wrong. He also felt that there was great baseball talent in the Negro Leagues. He wanted to build a championship Dodgers team. In 1945, Branch Rickey got the Dodgers board to agree to integrate.

Brooklyn Dodger scouts set out in search of Negro Leaguers who could compete in the Major Leagues. They narrowed their search to a few men. After careful research, Branch Rickey decided on Jackie Robinson. He told his scout, Clyde Sukeforth, to bring Jackie in for a meeting.

CHAPTER FIVE

The Meeting

When Jackie Robinson walked into Branch Rickey's office on August 28, 1945, he didn't know what to expect. Jackie met the steady gaze of a white man in his late sixties who wore wire-rimmed glasses, a bow tie, and held an unlit cigar between his fingers.

Branch Rickey knew the risk he was taking. If he and Jackie failed, it could take years for baseball to integrate. But if they were successful, they'd be changing more than the way baseball had been played since the late 1880s. They'd be changing America.

But was Jackie the right man? When faced with physical attacks and humiliation because he was black, would he hold back his temper? Would he strike back with his baseball skills and not his fists? Could anyone?

They stared at each other in silence until Branch Rickey asked, "Do you have a girl?"

Jackie told Mr. Rickey that he was engaged.

Branch Rickey leaned closer. His face was inches from Jackie. He twirled his cigar between his fingers.

"I've investigated you thoroughly, Robinson," Mr. Rickey said. "We can't fight our way through this . . . there's virtually nobody on our side. . . . And I'm afraid that many fans will be hostile. . . . We can win only if we can convince the world that I'm doing this because you're a great ballplayer and a fine gentleman." Mr. Rickey continued. "So there's more than just playing. I wish it meant only hits, runs, and errors—"

Jackie interrupted. "But it's the **box score** that really counts . . . that and that alone, isn't it?"

"It's all that *ought* to count," he answered. "But it isn't. Maybe one of these days it *will* be all that counts. . . . If you're a good enough man, we can make this a start in the right direction. But let me tell you, it's going to take an awful lot of courage."

The next few minutes were tough as Mr. Rickey tested Jackie. He had to be sure his twenty-six-year-old recruit knew what he'd be facing. Rickey called Robinson all kinds of racist names. He told Jackie that pitchers would be throwing balls at his head and fielders would spike him with their cleats. Mr. Rickey pounded on the desk with his fist to make his points.

"What will you do?" Branch demanded.

"Are you looking for a Negro who is afraid to fight back?" Jackie asked.

"I want a ballplayer with guts enough not to fight back," Rickey replied.

Jackie thought about what Branch Rickey was asking of him. He wanted the opportunity to play on the big-league level. He understood the pressure he'd be under. He'd have to perform on the field at the highest level while holding back his anger against the worst kind of insults and physical attacks. If they were successful, the doors would open for other black- and brown-skinned ball players. Jackie met Branch's hard stare and agreed, "I'll do it!"

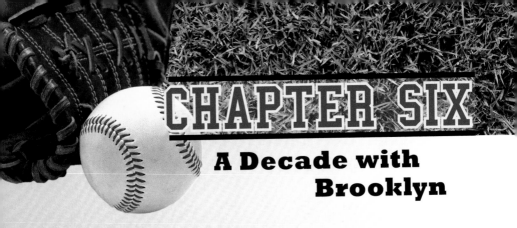

CHAPTER SIX

A Decade with Brooklyn

Jackie and Rachel were married on February 10, 1946, in Los Angeles, California.

Two weeks later, they began their journey to Jackie's first spring training in Florida. Jackie had been signed to the Montreal Royals, which was the farm team for the Brooklyn Dodgers. On the way to spring training for the Royals, Jackie and Rachel were bumped from a plane and forced to sit in the Jim Crow section on a long bus ride.

Jackie and Rachel arrive in Daytona Beach for spring training.

Wendell Smith, a black sports reporter, and Billy Rowe, a photographer, met Jackie and Rachel in Daytona Beach. A curious crowd had gathered to witness history. Wendell took the Robinsons to a private home within the black community. On the way, they passed the hotel where the white players stayed.

The Royals were training at a ballpark in Sanford, Florida, near Daytona Beach, for a week. On the third day, Mr. Rickey put in an emergency call to Wendell.

Jackie and Rachel were rushed out of town. Once they were safe, Wendell explained that an angry mob was headed toward the community where Rachel and Jackie were staying. The mob wanted to scare Jackie into quitting baseball.

Branch Rickey was waiting for Jackie and Rachel in Daytona. Jackie had one month to learn two new positions, first and second base, and make the team. They got to work.

"Take a lead!" Branch coached Jackie as he attempted to steal second. "Be bold! Make them worry," Mr. Rickey shouted as Jackie stole second base.

By the end of spring training, Jackie was ready. On March 17, 1946, he took to the field as a Montreal Royal!

It was a history-making moment. Jackie Robinson was the first black player in the twentieth century to take the field alongside whites in a scheduled exhibition game. The game drew record crowds. Black fans crowded into the Jim Crow section of the bleachers. Game on!

Branch Rickey signed two other black players, catcher Roy Campanella and pitcher Don Newcombe, to a farm team in New Hampshire. As Jackie and Rachel settled in Montreal for the season, they received a warm welcome, but in American cities Jackie faced abuse. In Syracuse, New York, a player from the opposing team threw a black cat onto the field as Jackie stepped into the batter's box. "Hey, Jackie, there's your cousin," the player shouted.

Jackie was steaming mad. He ignored the insult and hit a double. With the next batter, Jackie scored on a single. As he rounded third base, Jackie grinned over at the Syracuse bench. "I guess my cousin's happy now," he called out.

To combat the stress, Rachel created a warm and loving home. She and Jackie were expecting their first baby. "I had begun to think that I was married to a man with a destiny, someone who had been chosen for a great task, and I couldn't let him down," Rachel explained.

Jackie blossomed with their shared love. When the team traveled, he wrote Rachel letters. "I need you, Darling. You are my heart and soul," Jackie wrote.

By the end of the season, Jackie had a batting average of .349 with 40 stolen bases, and 100 team victories. The Montreal Royals won the International League Championship! After the game, the Canadian fans lifted Jackie up and carried him on their shoulders!

Jackie and Rachel returned to Los Angeles for the off-season. On November 18, 1946, Rachel gave birth to their first son, Jack Roosevelt Robinson, Jr.

CHAPTER SEVEN

Rookie of the Year!

At the start of the 1947 season, Major League Baseball was still segregated. On April 10, 1947, the Montreal Royals played the Brooklyn Dodgers in an exhibition game. After Jackie batted, the Dodgers offered to purchase his contract from the Montreal Royals. Jackie was handed his first number 42 Brooklyn uniform. He would be the first black

Jackie signs his contract with the Brooklyn Dodgers.

player in the National League, one of two divisions in Major League Baseball.

Not everyone was happy. In fact, a number of southern Dodgers players told Branch Rickey that they wouldn't play with a black man. Mr. Rickey said that was fine. He'd be happy to trade them. Pitcher Kirby Higbe accepted the trade.

Jackie's first official game with the Brooklyn franchise was April 15, 1947. He went hitless before a record crowd. Jackie recalled that he did a miserable job. He wrote, "There was an overflow crowd at Ebbets Field. If they expected any miracles out of Robinson, they were sadly disappointed." Jackie's slump deepened with only one base hit in the next four games.

Jackie's teammates were chilly to him. A few backed him. Some were openly against him. Off the field, Jackie was a loner.

On April 22, the Dodgers started a three-game series with Philadelphia. Jackie was still in a slump. The Phillies players taunted and tortured Jackie throughout the first game. Later, Jackie wrote, ". . . this day, of all the unpleasant days in my life, brought me nearer to cracking up than I ever had been. . . . I felt tortured and I tried just to play ball and ignore the insults. But it was really getting to me."

In Game Two of the Phillies series, one of Jackie's teammates, Eddie Stanky, jumped to his defense. "Listen, you yellow-bellied cowards," he yelled, "why don't you yell at somebody who can answer back?"

The next time the Dodgers and Phillies met was in Philadelphia. The town made it clear that they didn't want Jackie to show up. This time, some of the players greeted Jackie with bats pointed at him like they were machine guns.

Despite kicks, spikings, insults, physical attacks, and even death threats, Jackie grew stronger as a baseball player and as a man. Record crowds continued to fill stadiums across the country as Jackie turned his slump around and started to shine. Jackie's relationships with his teammates improved. He and Duke Snider ate dinner together.

At a game in Boston, the taunts were loud and angry. The fans heckled Dodger shortstop Pee Wee Reese. Pee Wee ignored the crowd. He walked over to Jackie, put his hand on his shoulder, and began talking to him. The crowd was shocked into silence. Pee Wee and Jackie remained friends for life.

On July 3, 1947, the Cleveland Indians signed Larry Doby of the Newark Eagles. The American League now had its first black player!

By the end of 1947, Jackie Robinson led the Dodgers in runs scored, singles, bunt hits, total bases, and stolen bases. With a season batting average of .297, Jackie was named Rookie of the Year for his performance on the field.

He was on the cover of *Time* magazine. And a national poll named Jack Roosevelt Robinson the second-most-popular person in America!

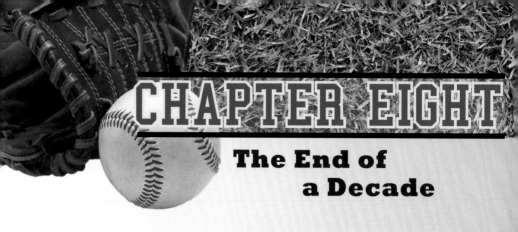

CHAPTER EIGHT

The End of a Decade

The 1948 season paled in comparison to 1947 and 1949. Jackie started off 1948 in a slump that didn't end until mid-June, when he hit his first grand slam. With Pee Wee Reese at shortstop and Jackie at second, the pair was an unstoppable double-play combination. By the end of the 1948 season, Jackie batted .296 with twelve home runs and eighty-five runs batted in. Jackie's fielding average for a second baseman was .983. He also led the league in being hit with seven pitched balls! And, for the first time, Jackie was thrown out of a game for heckling an umpire.

By 1949, the tension within Jackie had built up. As the 1949 season began, Branch Rickey freed Jackie to speak his mind! The fierce competitor returned to the field and Jackie had his best year of all. The racial tension was broken. Two black players, Roy Campanella and Don Newcombe, were brought up to the Dodgers from the farm team system. The

Jackie with Dodgers teammates Don Newcombe and Roy Campanella.

Dodgers won the National League pennant. And, Jackie was named Most Valuable Player.

The next year, Jackie and Rachel got their wish for a daughter. Sharon Annetta Robinson was born on January 13, 1950, in New York City. Three weeks after her birth, Sharon was on the set of *The Jackie Robinson Story*, starring Jackie Robinson as himself and Ruby Dee as Rachel. A movie producer had decided to make a movie about Jackie.

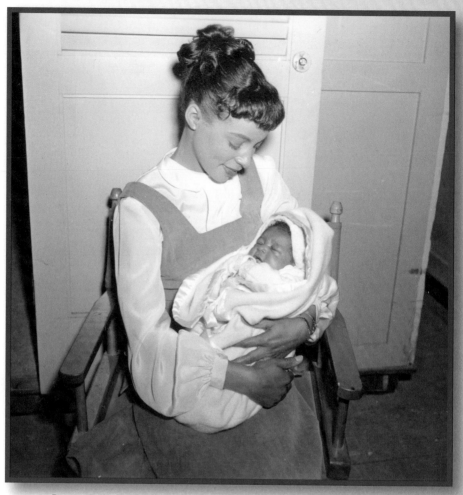

Actress Ruby Dee holds Sharon on the set of *The Jackie Robinson Story.*

After the filming, Jackie flew back east to spring training in Vero Beach, Florida. Rachel and the children stayed in California until the season began.

At three, Jackie Jr. started hanging around the baseball field. He'd swing the bat and fans would compare him to his father. For a while, Jackie Jr. loved the attention—then he started shying away from strangers.

Rachel's mother, Zellee Isum, and her grandmother, Annetta Jones, flew east from California to visit.

At the end of the 1950 season, Walter O'Malley had taken Branch Rickey's place as president of the Brooklyn Dodgers. Walter O'Malley made it known that he did not like Branch Rickey. Jackie, who was loyal to Branch Rickey, didn't take the change well. The 1951, 1952, and 1953 seasons were difficult. The more outspoken Robinson became, the less he was liked by the sportswriters. Jackie finally had it out with a reporter from New York's *Daily News*. Jackie once wrote, "I was infinitely more interested in being respected as a man than in being liked."

The Robinsons' third baby, David, was born on May 14, 1952. With their family complete, Jack and Rachel had begun to search for a new house. They'd been living in a three-bedroom home in St. Albans, New York. Their community had other famous athletes and entertainers in it. Jackie wanted more privacy and a house with more land.

Their search was complicated by housing rules that kept blacks from buying in certain neighborhoods. Andrea Simon and a number of **liberal** builders, real-estate brokers, and ministers from Stamford,

The Robinsons' first winter in their new home.

Connecticut, stepped in. With help, Rachel and Jackie found their dream property. The house sat on a hill overlooking a beautiful lake. It was framed by woods. They moved into their new home in 1955.

That same year, the Brooklyn Dodgers finally beat the New York Yankees in a seven-game Series. It was the first World Championship for the Brooklyn Dodgers!

After the 1956 season, the Brooklyn Dodgers unloaded a number of their older players. Jackie had begun planning his own retirement when he was traded to another baseball team, the New York Giants. Instead of switching teams, he broke the news of his retirement in the January 1957 issue of *Look* magazine.

CHAPTER NINE

A Lasting Legacy

Jackie Robinson's post-baseball years were dedicated to family, work, the **civil rights movement**, and politics. In the early years, Jackie was a vice president for the popular coffee company Chock Full o' Nuts.

He also traveled the country raising money for the civil rights organization the National Association for the Advancement of Colored People (NAACP).

Later, Jackie entered New York State politics with Nelson Rockefeller and went on to national politics. He marched alongside Dr. Martin Luther King, Jr., and many other civil rights leaders.

In 1963, Jackie and Rachel hosted a jazz concert at their home to raise money for Dr. Martin Luther King, Jr.

He wrote columns, books, and letters to presidents advocating for equal rights. Jackie was a television analyst for baseball, a radio personality, and the cofounder of the Freedom National Bank. But one of his biggest achievements came in 1962, when he was inducted into the Baseball Hall of Fame. Jackie had asked sportswriters to vote solely on his career statistics, and not consider his breaking the color barrier. And Jackie Robinson did have some impressive numbers. Batting average: .311. Hits: 1,518. Home runs: 137. Runs batted in: 734. Stolen bases: 197. Steals of home: 19. Rookie of the Year: 1947. MVP: 1949.

Jackie with Branch and Rachel at his Baseball Hall of Fame induction.

In 1963, the Robinson family was on the Mall in Washington, D.C., for Dr. King's famous "I Have a Dream" speech. After that, Jackie and Rachel opened their home for jazz concerts to raise money for Dr. King. They continued to host jazz concerts for the civil rights movement for years to come.

In Jackie's home life, the lake became the center of family activity. In the summer, Jackie Jr., Sharon, and David swam, fished, rowed a boat, and captured sunbathing turtles. In the spring, they watched tadpoles turn into frogs. Winter was reserved for figure skating and ice hockey. Baseball and football were played on the front lawn. The woods offered a place to explore, create, and hide. A horse named Diamond taught responsibility and risk-taking.

Rachel went back to graduate school at New York University and went on to work as a psychiatric nurse. The schools Jackie Jr., Sharon, and David attended became integrated, and the children faced a variety of tough issues as they entered adolescence. Jackie Jr. served in Vietnam and died in a tragic car accident at twenty-four.

After retiring from baseball, Jackie was diagnosed with diabetes. Then, in 1972, Jackie Robinson died after a heart attack. He was fifty-three. In his eulogy, Reverend Jesse Jackson told the packed Riverside

Church that "Jackie's body was a temple of God . . . an instrument of peace."

Jackson continued describing Jackie's growth from champion to hero. He said, "A champion is lifted onto the shoulders of the people; a hero lifts the people on his shoulders." A champion is often forgotten. A hero lives on.

Jackie Robinson is an American hero. His legacy lives on through his family, Major League Baseball, the Jackie Robinson Foundation, and generations of kids who study his life, character, baseball career, and impact on America.

The Baseball Hall of Fame changed his plaque to include his pioneering efforts in breaking the color barrier. It reads, "Displayed tremendous courage and poise in 1947 when he integrated the modern major leagues in the face of intense adversity."

Rachel Robinson founded the Jackie Robinson Foundation in 1973. It provides scholarships and leadership development to thousands of young people across America. In 1997, Major League Baseball retired Jackie's number, 42, throughout every team. And April 15 was named Jackie Robinson Day!

Jackie and Rachel's daughter, Sharon, became a nurse midwife, author, and educational consultant to Major League Baseball. Their son David became a

Mets players and coaches wore number 42
on Jackie Robinson Day.

Members of the Robinson family with Jackie Robinson Foundation scholars and board members.

coffee grower in Tanzania, East Africa. Combined, Jackie Jr., Sharon, and David had twelve children.

Perhaps Jackie Robinson left all of us his greatest legacy when he reminded us, "A life is not important except for the impact it has on other lives."

Sharon and David share Jackie Robinson Day
with their mother.

GLOSSARY

box score: the statistics for a baseball game

civil rights movement: movement in the United States beginning in the 1960s that fought for the equal rights of all people regardless of the their race, gender, or religion

court martial: a trial for members of the military made up by a court of officers

draft: to make someone join the military

farm team: a sports team in a lower or minor league affiliated with one in a higher league

insubordination: an act of disobedience to authority

Jim Crow laws: laws enforced between 1874–1975 to separate the white and black races in the American South

lettering: winning an award for outstanding athletic achievement while attending school

liberal: in favor of political change and reform

segregation: the act or process of keeping people or groups apart

sharecropper: a farmer who works on the land for the owner in return for a share of the value of the crop

AUTHOR Q+A

Q: What was different about writing this book versus other books you've written about your dad?

A: This was the first time I've written a book about my family in third person. It felt strange at first, but telling the story in third person offered me new insight and enhanced perspective.

Q: Did you learn anything new?

A: I had a few surprises with this book. For example, I knew that my great grandparents were enslaved. I learned that when freed, they were land owners. This was a very cool fact. I also clarified my father's army court-martial.

Q: What is the one thing that you'd like young readers to know about your father?

A: That Jackie Robinson lived his life according to his motto: "A life is not important except in the impact it has on others."

Q: When you're not writing what do you enjoy doing?

A: Swimming, going on long walks with my dogs, hanging out with my grandchildren, and going to baseball games!

Q: What is your favorite type of book to read?

A: I like to read fiction.

Q: Who's your favorite Major League Baseball team?

A: That's a tough one. . . . Since I work for the commissioner of Major League Baseball, I'm not supposed to have favorites. However, given my family's history with the Dodgers, I'm given some slack. Go Dodgers!

Q: Tell us about the Jackie Robinson Foundation.

A: JRF is a scholarship and leadership-development organization that was founded in 1973 by my mother. We've supported over 1,500 scholars and 98 percent of our scholars graduate.

Q: Are there any new Jackie Robinson projects on the horizon?

A: We're thrilled that in April 2013, *42*, the film, will open in movie theaters across the country! Check it out!